AFGHANISTAN

...in Pictures

Visual Geography Series®

AFGHANISTAN

...in Pictures

Prepared by
Geography Department

Lerner Publications Company
Minneapolis

12422

Independent Picture Service

A young Afghan woman carries her sister and a carefully tied bundle with ease.

This is an all-new edition of the Visual Geography Series. Previous editions have been published by Sterling Publishing Company, New York City, and some of the original textual information has been retained. New photographs, maps, charts, captions, and updated information have been added. The text has been entirely reset in 10/12 Century Textbook.

LIBRARY OF CONGRESS CATALOGING-IN-PUBLICATION DATA

Afghanistan in pictures.

(Visual geography series)
  Rev. ed. of: Afghanistan in pictures / by Camille Mirepoix.
  Includes index.
  Summary: An introduction to the geography, history, government, people, and economy of this landlocked country with a long history of warfare and conquest.
  1. Afghanistan. [1. Afghanistan] I. Mirepoix, Camille. Afghanistan in pictures. II. Lerner Publications Company. Geography Dept. III. Title. IV. Series: Visual geography series (Minneapolis, Minn.)
DS351.5.A345   1989   958'.1   88-13587
ISBN 0-8225-1849-X (lib. bdg.)

International Standard Book Number: 0-8225-1849-X
Library of Congress Card Catalog Number: 88-13587

VISUAL GEOGRAPHY SERIES®

Publisher
Harry Jonas Lerner
Associate Publisher
Nancy M. Campbell
Senior Editor
Mary M. Rodgers
Editor
Gretchen Bratvold
Assistant Editors
Dan Filbin
Kathleen S. Heidel
Photo Researcher
Karen A. Sirvaitis
Editorial/Photo Assistant
Marybeth Campbell
Consultants/Contributors
Isaac Eshel
Dr. Ruth F. Hale
Sandra K. Davis
Designer
Jim Simondet
Cartographer
Carol F. Barrett
Indexer
Sylvia Timian
Production Manager
Richard J. Hannah

Independent Picture Service

Laborers on an Afghan farm enjoy a joke during harvesttime.

Acknowledgments

Title page photo courtesy of Center for Afghanistan Studies.

Elevation contours adapted from *The Times Atlas of the World*, seventh comprehensive edition (New York: Times Books, 1985).

1 2   3   4   5   6   7   8   9   10 98 97 96 95 94 93 92 91 90 89

Simple dwellings sit among the hills of Afghanistan's mountainous areas, which extend through the middle of the country.

Contents

SOVIET UNION

IRAN

WAKHAN CORRIDOR

CHINA

Amu Darya Bridge

Pipeline

BALKH
Balkh

Amu Darya

KUNDUZ

Shibarghan
Mazar-i-Sharif

Kunduz

BADAKHSHAN

JOWZJAN

R.

Baghlan
Pul-i-Khumri

FARYAB

Band-i-Amir

BAGHLAN

Panjsher R.

Gulbahar

KAPISA

BAMIAN

Charikar

Herat

Hari Rud

Bamian

KABUL

Mahipar
Naghlu

Jalalabad

Kabul R.

Peshawar

NANGARHAR

Ghazni

PAKISTAN

Arghandab R.

Tarnak R.

PAKTIA

Lake Helmand

Dori R.

Kandahar

Helmand R.

GAWD-I-ZIRREH

IRAN

AFGHANISTAN

N
↑

- - - Province Boundaries

——— Roads

0   50   100   150 Miles

0   50   100   150 Kilometers

40°   60°   40°

20°

20°

20°

40°   60°

INDIAN OCEAN

MIDDLE EAST
AFGHANISTAN

0   500 Miles

0   500 Kilometers

METRIC CONVERSION CHART
To Find Approximate Equivalents

WHEN YOU KNOW:	MULTIPLY BY:	TO FIND:
AREA		
acres	0.41	hectares
square miles	2.59	square kilometers
CAPACITY		
gallons	3.79	liters
LENGTH		
feet	30.48	centimeters
yards	0.91	meters
miles	1.61	kilometers
MASS (weight)		
pounds	0.45	kilograms
tons	0.91	metric tons
VOLUME		
cubic yards	0.77	cubic meters
TEMPERATURE		
degrees Fahrenheit	0.56 (*after* subtracting 32)	degrees Celsius

Clutching a homemade water jug, a young Afghan makes her way from the communal well to her village. Only 10 percent of Afghanistan's population have access to safe drinking water.

Introduction

Landlocked Afghanistan lies in southwestern Asia and is composed of high mountains, large deserts, and a few fertile valleys and plains. Most Afghans are Muslims (followers of the Islamic religion), and Islam unites the many ethnic groups that make up the population. Nevertheless, each community retains its particular language and customs.

Because of its location at the crossroads of ancient Asian trade routes, Afghanistan has a long history of warfare and conquest. Persians, Greeks, Mongols, British, and Russians have participated at various times in the invasions and strife that have frequently disrupted Afghanistan.

In 1979 Soviet troops arrived in the country to prop up the pro-Soviet Afghan

Courtesy of Center for Afghanistan Studies

Islamic tradition urges women to hide themselves from public view.

government. This event has caused a violent, anti-Soviet guerrilla movement to arise within Afghanistan. The struggle pits the Soviet-supported Afghan government against the Islamic *mujahedeen* (holy warriors).

Millions of Afghans have fled to nearby Pakistan and Iran, and thousands of others —soldiers, civilians, and guerrillas—have been killed in the fighting. In April 1988 the leaders of Afghanistan and Pakistan signed an agreement, which settled some differences between the two nations. The document led to the gradual withdrawal of most of the Soviet troops. But conflicts between the mujahedeen and the Afghan government continue to endanger the nation's immediate prospects for peace.

Courtesy of A. Hollmann/UNHCR

Afghan refugees—who, since 1980, have fled the conflict in their homeland—cluster near temporary shelters at a camp in eastern Iran.

Photo by Daniel H. Condit

Snow-dusted and jagged, the mountains of the Hindu Kush rise to heights of over 20,000 feet above sea level in Afghanistan and Pakistan.

1) The Land

Located near the center of the Asian continent, Afghanistan is a landlocked country, and over half of its area consists of high plateaus and mountains. The mountains of the Hindu Kush and other ranges extend across the country from southwest to northeast. North and west of the mountains are fertile valleys and plains, and desert areas lie in the south.

With 251,773 square miles of territory, Afghanistan is slightly smaller than the state of Texas. The Soviet Union lies to the north, Iran borders Afghanistan to the west, and Pakistan is situated to the south and east. A narrow strip of northeastern territory—called the Wakhan Corridor—borders Jammu and Kashmir (a region that both Pakistan and India claim) and a small portion of China.

Topography

Geographers disagree on the regional breakdown of Afghanistan's landscape. But the country may generally be divided into three areas—the northern plains, the central mountain ranges, and the southern lowlands.

9

NORTHERN PLAINS

The plains of northern Afghanistan border the Soviet Union and include elevated plateaus and low hills. Melting snows and local rivers water the region, and farmers build simple canals that direct moisture to fields where it is most needed. The fertile soil in the plains supports extensive grasslands on which Afghan herders graze their sheep. Another feature of the area are valleys that contain productive farms. Yet some aspects of the landscape show signs of the recent conflicts within the country. Families have fled northeastern sections of the region, where fighting is heavy, leaving farms and pastureland untended.

CENTRAL MOUNTAINS

Dominating Afghanistan's topography are the nation's central mountain ranges, which fan out in a wide expanse in the mid-

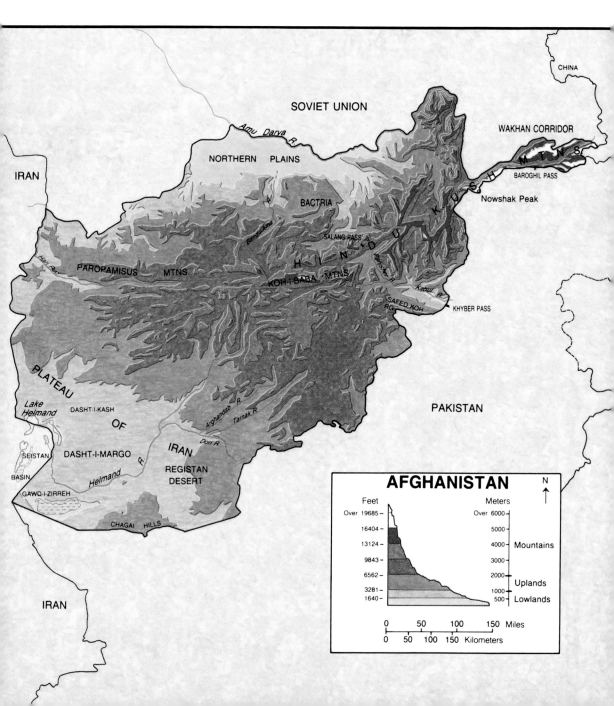

The plains of northern Afghanistan afford these nomadic herders nourishing grasses for their livestock.

dle of the country. The Paropamisus Mountains, which climb to heights of over 11,000 feet above sea level, lie in western Afghanistan. As they reach central Afghanistan, these mountains blend into the Koh-i-Baba range, whose peaks rise to almost 17,000 feet. The Koh-i-Baba Mountains form the southwestern portion of the Hindu Kush —the main mountain range in Afghanistan.

The Hindu Kush extends from the middle of Afghanistan, through the Wakhan Corridor, to the Soviet Union. In Afghanistan the highest summit is Nowshak Peak, which rises to 24,557 feet near the nation's northeastern border with Pakistan. The Safed Koh Range, an offshoot of the Hindu Kush, is shared by Afghanistan and Pakistan. The peaks of this range reach heights of nearly 16,000 feet.

The Koh-i-Baba Mountains overshadow a freshly harvested field in a valley near the ancient city of Bamian, which is located in northeastern Afghanistan.

Although the steep terrain of the central highlands hinders travel, narrow routes—called passes—through the ranges have provided thoroughfares for merchants, invaders, and refugees. The Khyber Pass, for example, gives access to Pakistan through the Safed Koh Range. Another intermountain route is the Baroghil Pass, which crosses the Hindu Kush and links northern Pakistan with the Wakhan Corridor.

SOUTHERN LOWLANDS

The landscape of the southwestern lowlands rarely rises more than 3,000 feet above sea level, except in the far south, where Pakistan's Chagai Hills mark the border with Afghanistan. Although the Helmand River travels through southern Afghanistan on its way to Iran, most of the land in the south is desert or semidesert.

The Registan Desert covers an extensive corner of southeastern Afghanistan, and two smaller deserts—the Dasht-i-Margo and Dasht-i-Kash—lie north of the Helmand. To the extreme southwest is the Gawd-i-Zirreh—a marshland that occasionally overflows with water in the wet season and merges with Lake Helmand.

The deserts and marshland are part of the Plateau of Iran, a landscape feature that Afghanistan, Pakistan, and Iran share. The entire plateau covers an area of one million square miles, fewer than half of which lie within Afghanistan.

Rivers

Afghanistan's rivers provide water for irrigation, although some waterways dry up in the summer. The Helmand—the longest inland river in Afghanistan—originates in the Koh-i-Baba Mountains and flows south for 870 miles before emptying into Lake Helmand. The lake lies in the Seistan Basin—a swampy region between Iran and Afghanistan. The Helmand's tributaries—the Arghandab and the Tarnak—provide abundant water for irrigation.

The Kabul River also begins in the Koh-i-Baba, and its 400-mile course runs through Afghanistan before flowing north of the Khyber Pass into Pakistan. Form-

Independent Picture Service

Narrow, twisting paths—called passes—snake through Afghanistan's rugged landscape, giving access to otherwise unreachable parts of the country.

An aerial view of the Band-i-Amir River and its tributaries shows their courses as they flow through the provinces of Jowzjan and Balkh in northern Afghanistan.

ing part of Afghanistan's boundary with the Soviet Union, the Amu Darya River, as well as its tributaries, are fed by the snows of the Hindu Kush. The river eventually winds its way north to empty into the Aral Sea, which lies in the Turkmen Soviet Socialist Republic (part of the Soviet Union).

The 700-mile-long Hari Rud originates in the Koh-i-Baba Mountains of central Afghanistan and drains the fertile valley around Herat. The Hari's course flows west through the Paropamisus Mountains and turns north to form part of the boundary between Afghanistan and Iran. The river eventually dries up in the deserts of the Turkmen S.S.R.

The Panjsher River churns its way through the Hindu Kush to join the Kabul River.

Flora and Fauna

Although thick vegetation grows in Afghanistan's low valleys, the country's high mountains are generally treeless and windswept. Large evergreens, such as cedars, pines, and firs, exist on the mountainsides, and acacia, walnut, and oak trees flourish on the lower slopes. Wildflowers—including

13

wild roses and honeysuckle—thrive in the mountains and grasslands of the north. Date palms survive in the south, where scrub vegetation predominates, and herbs of the daisy, mint, and carrot families are abundant.

Single-humped dromedary camels commonly live in the plains, and two-humped Bactrian camels inhabit mountain areas. The highlands host snow leopards, wolves, foxes, antelope, ibex (wild goats), markhors (mountain sheep), and brown bears. Afghanistan is famous for a breed of hunting dog—called an Afghan hound—that has long been raised in the northern regions of the country. Migratory birds—such as snipes, pelicans, herons, and sandpipers —visit Afghanistan and flourish alongside native pigeons, partridges, pheasants, and woodcocks.

An Afghan herder leads his brightly draped Bactrian (two-humped) camel to grazing land. Bactrian camels can go without water for many days because they get moisture from plants as well as from water. The camel's humps store fat—not water—for use as energy when food is scarce. As the animal uses the stored fat, its humps shrink until food and rest restore the humps to their normal shape.

Many Afghans cherish their horses, especially those that are ridden in games of *buzkashi.* This daring sport can involve dozens of skilled horsemen in pursuit of the same object—the body of a headless calf—which they carry to a goal.

Native doves flock to the courtyard of the Blue Mosque (an Islamic place of prayer) in the city of Mazar-i-Sharif.

During springtime, a horse grazes contentedly on fresh grasses in the hills of Paktia, a province in eastern Afghanistan.

Climate

Situated between the wet monsoon zone of India and arid central Asia, Afghanistan has a dry and sunny climate, with extremely hot summers and very cold winters.

Because the nation is landlocked, no nearby bodies of water exist to moderate its climate.

Cold air masses from Siberia enter the country from the north, bringing snow and cold temperatures in winter. The effects of southern Asia's summer monsoons (seasonal, rain-bearing winds) are felt in the warm months, when heavy rains occur in the Hindu Kush. Strong southwestern winds are also a feature of the summer months in western Afghanistan.

Throughout Afghanistan, extremes in temperature are common, and a day that starts out at 40° F can reach 100° F by noon. In the northern plains, temperatures average about 38° F in January (the coldest month) and 90° F in July (the hottest month). Summer temperatures occasionally are much warmer, and the fertile valleys have recorded highs of 110° to 120° F. Annual rainfall in the region averages only about seven inches, half of which comes as snow.

Temperatures in the central highlands reach about 25° F in January and about 75° F in July. This region receives heavy snow, which remains on the highest mountains throughout the year. Lower elevations get about 15 inches of rain annually.

In winter, snow clogs Salang Pass—a route through the Hindu Kush. Modern equipment is used to clear the drifts so that traffic is not interrupted.

The southwestern lowlands are mainly desert, although some areas are watered by the Helmand River. The region's temperatures average about 35° F in January and about 85° F in July. Precipitation ranges from one to eight inches per year.

Cities

Located west of the Koh-i-Baba Mountains, Afghanistan's capital city of Kabul lies along the banks of the Kabul River. In ancient times Kabul was a main stop for trade caravans from China, and the city eventually became the largest and most important urban center in Afghanistan. Inhabited for about 2,500 years, the city became the capital of Afghanistan in 1776. By 1987 the city's population had reached over two million, a figure that included large numbers of Afghan refugees who had fled the war in the countryside.

Old and new styles of living blend in Kabul, where some houses in older neighborhoods have metal roofs and thick walls made of mud bricks. Newer sections

The brick dwellings of an old section of Kabul—the capital of Afghanistan—stretch toward the Koh-i-Baba Mountains in the distance.

17

of the capital boast wide, tree-lined avenues where modern businesses, government offices, and university buildings are located. Kabul is one of Afghanistan's main transportation hubs for export products, which include carpets and dried fruits. The city also has factories that produce plastics, textiles, furniture, and wine.

Kandahar (population 209,000), the second largest city in Afghanistan, is the commercial center of the nation. Lying in a fertile plain in southern Afghanistan, the city is the headquarters of several industrial projects that use the region's agricultural products as raw materials. Fruit and canning operations exist, and a textile mill weaves locally grown cotton into cloth.

Because Herat (population 200,000) lies near the Iranian border, this city in western Afghanistan has become the gateway for refugees fleeing the Afghan conflict. Once a depot for silks and gems from India, China, and Arabia, Herat now makes rugs and exports fruits. Since its founding in the third century B.C., the city has been invaded many times. Muslim armies took Herat in the seventh century A.D., and the Mongol conqueror Timur made the city his capital in 1381, transforming it into a center of Islamic art and learning.

Mazar-i-Sharif (population 150,000) is the main urban area of northern Afghanistan. The focus of commercial activity in the Afghan Turkistan region, Mazar-i-Sharif is also an important place of Islamic pilgrimage. The city's fifteenth-century mosque (Islamic place of prayer) is believed to hold the tomb of Ali, one of Islam's most important religious leaders and the son-in-law of the prophet Muhammad, who founded the religion.

Herat's Friday Mosque—originally built in 1200, when the Ghurid family of rulers controlled the city—is decorated with geometric patterns. Bombing during the Afghan war destroyed parts of the mosque.

Photo © Ric Ergenbright

Afghanistan's ethnic diversity is partly the result of the many different peoples who have conquered, escaped to, or fought in the country. These modern-day Afghan refugees line up to receive food at a camp in Iran.

2) History and Government

Afghanistan's landlocked location has often trapped it between competing powers in southern, central, and western Asia. Conquering armies passed through the region, and refugee populations from neighboring areas streamed into Afghanistan, adding to the nation's ethnic diversity. At times, Afghanistan was the battleground on which conflicting empires pursued their quest for regional control.

Archaeological evidence shows that the earliest settlements in the region began about 3000 B.C. in Afghanistan's portion of the Plateau of Iran. Local peoples usually were nomadic herders, but eventu-

ally they developed permanent farming villages.

By about 1500 B.C. some of the scattered villages had developed into small urban centers, especially in northern and southern Afghanistan. Among the earliest known groups were the Bactrians, who inhabited Bactria, an area in northern Afghanistan that lies between the Amu Darya River and the Hindu Kush.

Early Invasions

Extensive records of Afghanistan's history begin in about 550 B.C., when the region came under the authority of the Achaemenid dynasty (family of rulers) of Persia (modern Iran). Under the Achaemenids, Afghanistan was made up of several provinces, called satrapies, which included Bactria in the north and Aria near modern Herat. The Achaemenids subdued the local populations with considerable difficulty, and Persian troops were stationed throughout the Hindu Kush to control the area.

Disagreements about the succession to the Persian throne began in the fourth century B.C. and weakened Persian control of outlying areas. In addition, a young Greek general named Alexander of Macedon (later called Alexander the Great) saw this period of instability as an opportunity to invade Persia. Beginning in about 334 B.C., Alexander moved his conquering armies eastward, taking control of Persian lands during his long marches. The satrapy of Bactria fell after a series of fierce battles between 330 and 327 B.C.

A silver tetradrachm coin – issued in 323 B.C., the year Alexander the Great died – shows the head of Hercules on the front *(top)*. The back of the coin *(bottom)* depicts Zeus (the strongest of the Greek gods) enthroned, holding a royal scepter and an eagle. The Greek lettering translates as "Alexander the king."

A mosaic from the fourth century B.C. illustrates Alexander the Great in battle. The confrontation between Alexander and Darius III, the last king of the Achaemenid ruling family, signaled the end of this Persian dynasty. After defeating Darius, Alexander led his troops east into Bactria (northern Afghanistan), which was absorbed into his growing empire in 327 B.C.

The profile *(left)* of the Parthian king Mithradates II appears on a silver coin minted during his reign (123–88 B.C.). The back of the coin *(right)* shows the king on his throne, with "Mithradates the king" inscribed in Greek letters around the rim. In addition to Persian lands, Mithradates ruled parts of northern and western Afghanistan.

To quiet some of the local satraps (administrators of satrapies), who strongly resisted being absorbed by the Greeks, Alexander married Roxana, the daughter of the satrap of Bactria. He and his troops continued eastward, conquering a region along the banks of the Indus River in what is now Pakistan. A near mutiny of Alexander's troops in 325 B.C. forced Alexander to lead them back to Greece, and he left his most trusted generals in charge of the newly conquered areas.

Seleucids, Bactrians, and Parthians

A mere two years later, Alexander died without declaring an heir, and his generals divided his vast realm. The Greek general Seleucus took control of the Persian lands, which included Bactria, and founded the Seleucid dynasty. Large numbers of Greek colonists came to the Hindu Kush, and, as a result, Greek culture flourished in the area.

Seleucid control lasted for less than a century, however, and Bactria revolted in about 250 B.C. The Greek-influenced Bactrians established a strong state that later stretched west into Persia, east into India, and south as far as the Arabian Sea. The Greco-Bactrian kingdom lasted for about 150 years, until the Parthians—a central Asian people—conquered the Persian Empire and took control of northern and western Afghanistan.

Other powers also competed for land in the region. The Saka, another central Asian group, controlled southwestern Afghanistan, and rulers of the Maurya dynasty in eastern India extended their holdings as far west as Afghanistan. Maurya rulers introduced the Bactrians to the Buddhist religion, which the philosopher Gautama Buddha had founded in India in the sixth century B.C.

Kushan Empire

Afghanistan was only a remote province of the Persian and Mauryan empires. Another powerful group—the Kushan, who originated in China—invaded the region in about A.D. 50. The Kushan defeated the Parthians and the Saka in the west, united Bactria with Sogdiana (a region to the north), and extended their rule over Kashmir and the Kabul River Valley. They

Photo by © Ric Ergenbright

Huge statues representing Gautama Buddha—who founded the Buddhist religion—rise among the sandstone cliffs of the Bamian Valley. This region of northern Afghanistan was a center of Buddhist learning and culture in the first few centuries of the Christian era.

traded widely, for they controlled part of the Silk Road—a trade route that passed from China through the Middle East to Europe. The Kushan also served as brokers in commercial exchanges between the Roman Empire and India.

The Kushan, who followed the Buddhist religion, fostered Buddhism in Afghanistan. Under Kushan influence, Buddhist philosophy and art mingled with the Greek culture that had been introduced earlier. Eastern Afghanistan, in particular, became a hub of Buddhist culture. Bamian, a city

north of the Koh-i-Baba Mountains, contains massive statues that are examples of Buddhism's presence in Afghanistan.

The greatest of the Kushan rulers was Kaniska, who ruled from about A.D. 78 to A.D. 103 and who established Perushapure (near modern Peshawar, Pakistan) as his capital. He spent the summer months in Kapisa, north of what is now Kabul. Kaniska supported the arts, encouraged Buddhist learning, and strengthened commercial ties along the trade routes that ran through Afghanistan.

New Invaders

By about the third century A.D., the Kushan Empire had split into small independent kingdoms. These realms became prey first to the Sasanians from Persia and then to forces of the Gupta Empire centered in eastern India. In the early eighth century armies from Arabia—fired by the Islamic religion, which the prophet Muhammad had founded in about A.D. 610 —arrived in Afghanistan.

After defeating the Kushan troops, the rulers of the expanding Islamic realm added Afghanistan to their holdings. During the next 200 years, local populations slowly converted to the Islamic religion and developed semi-independent dynasties. As a result, control of Afghanistan rapidly changed hands as competing realms rose and fell in the region.

Ghaznavids and Ghurids

By the end of the tenth century, the Ghaznavid dynasty had established itself in Ghazni, a city situated southwest of Kabul. In 999 Mahmud of Ghazna became ruler of the region and led annual raiding expeditions into India. Mahmud's twofold aim was to convert local populations to Islam and to take treasures back to Ghazni. His realm eventually extended as far east as present-day Punjab, India, and beyond the Amu Darya River to the north. The Ghaznavid Empire also included all of the Hindu Kush.

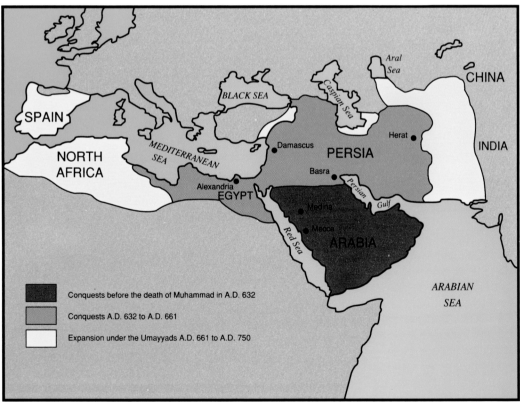

Conquests before the death of Muhammad in A.D. 632

Conquests A.D. 632 to A.D. 661

Expansion under the Umayyads A.D. 661 to A.D. 750

Artwork by Mindy A. Rabin

Armies made up of Muslims—followers of the Islamic faith that began in Arabia—invaded Afghanistan in the early eighth century A.D. The region was added to the holdings of the Umayyad dynasty, which ruled conquered Islamic territories until 750.

After Mahmud's death in 1030, the realm came under attack by Turkish as well as local groups. By 1186, under the leadership of Muhammad Ghuri, troops of the Ghurid dynasty—centered in northwestern Afghanistan—completely overthrew the Ghaznavids. The Ghurids spread the Islamic religion, not only in their own holdings but also on the Indian subcontinent (a region in southern Asia that consists of India, Pakistan, Nepal, and Bangladesh).

Ghurid control lasted less than a century, however, before it began to falter under the sweeping attacks of central Asian forces commanded by the Mongol warrior Genghis Khan. In time, his empire stretched from eastern China to the Caspian Sea (in the Soviet Union).

Mongols

In 1220 the Mongols invaded Afghanistan, plundered its cities, and massacred its people. They destroyed Bactria and burned down Herat and Bamian. These attacks wiped out nearly all evidence of Buddhism in Afghanistan. They could not dislodge the Islamic religion, however, which had taken firmer hold in the region than had Buddhism.

Genghis Khan died in 1227, and his descendants continued to raid the Indian subcontinent. But the Mongol Empire was fragmented, and semi-independent dynasties emerged. One of these was the Tajik dynasty, which rose to prominence in Herat and ruled until a new conqueror, Timur the Lame, took over the entire region.

A descendant of Genghis Khan, Timur (also known as Tamerlane) conquered northern Afghanistan in about 1380. By the end of the fourteenth century, his empire stretched from India to Turkey. Timur died in 1405, and his successors established the Timurid dynasty in Herat. Supporters of Islamic culture, Timurid rulers developed their capital city into a great

Courtesy of W. Campbell-Notar

In the eleventh century the Ghaznavid leader Mahmud built this pillar in Ghazni to commemorate his military victories.

Photo by Daniel H. Condit

One of the partially ruined Buddhist statues at Bamian shows the effects of Mongol attacks in the thirteenth century.

Courtesy of James Ford Bell Library, University of Minnesota

The Mongol warrior Timur the Lame conquered Afghanistan in about 1380. He laid the foundations of the Timurid dynasty, which was centered in Herat.

Courtesy of Center for Afghanistan Studies

The richness and variety of Islamic architectural designs are evident in the facade of a fifteenth-century tomb.

center of art and learning. Commerce and culture flourished until the early sixteenth century, when yet another Mongol group invaded Afghanistan.

A descendant of Genghis Khan and Timur, Zahir-ud-Din Muhammad (called Babur by his followers) took Kabul in 1504. He favored the city above others in his conquests, and he is buried near it. His invasion of Delhi, India, in 1526 laid the foundations of the Mughal Empire. (The name Mughal is derived from the word *Mongol.*)

Competition for Afghan Territory

Since the center of the Mughal Empire was in Delhi, the lands in Afghanistan were distant provinces and became easy prey for invading powers. For two centuries the Mughals, the Safavids from Persia, and the Uzbek from what is now the Soviet Union competed for control of Afghanistan. By the mid-eighteenth century, western Afghanistan had fallen under the rule of Persia, and the Uzbek controlled northern Afghanistan. Eastern Afghanistan remained a remote province of the Mughal Empire.

Under the leadership of an Afghan general named Mir Wais Khan, western Afghan peoples succeeded in overthrowing the Persians. The Persians, however, regained parts of Afghanistan under their king Nader Shah. When a member of the king's guard assassinated Nader Shah in 1747, Afghan leaders again asserted their independence.

Rise of Ahmad Shah

Although Afghanistan's population had often resisted foreign invaders, it was not unified into a single people. Instead, many separate ethnic communities thrived, taking up arms to fight would-be conquerors who arrived in their territories. Sometimes Afghans protected their lands—and added to their personal wealth—by joining their conquerors, who paid them well and who gave them opportunities to loot captured cities. The most populous Afghan group was the Pathans, who were also called Pushtuns or Pakhtuns. Tajiks and several peoples descended from the Uzbek and Turkomans also lived in the region.

One of the most able Afghan fighters was Ahmad Khan, a member of the Abdali Pathans (a Pathan subgroup) and the son of an important Abdali leader. Ahmad had rebelled against the Persian monarch Nader Shah in about 1735 and had gained a reputation as a skilled commander and horseman.

After Nader Shah's assassination, Ahmad sought to unite Afghan peoples against further foreign domination. Along with other Pathans in his clan, he attended a meeting to choose a leader of the Pathan people. The Pathans selected Ahmad as shah (king) in 1747. Ahmad Shah became known as Durr-e-Durran (pearl of pearls), and thereafter the Abdali Pathans were called the Durrani.

Ahmad Shah's Reign

Ahmad Shah spent much of his 26-year reign subduing new territories, maintaining control over them, and suppressing rebellions among his own people. He fought the successor of Nader Shah for control of Herat, taking over part of eastern Persia—the present-day province of Khorasan—in the process.

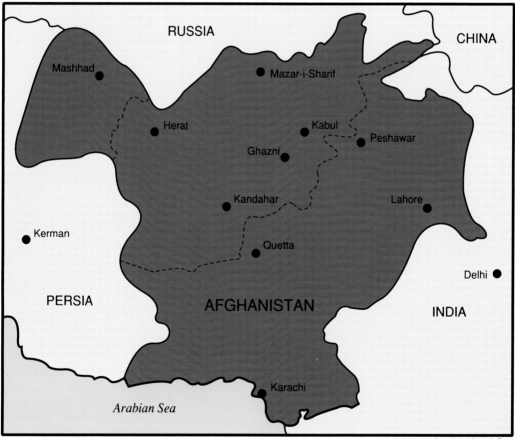

Artwork by Mindy A. Rabin

At its height in the mid-eighteenth century, the empire of Ahmad Shah stretched into Persia and India. (The dotted line indicates Afghanistan's current boundaries.)

After several decades of unstable rule, Dost Mohammad Khan took over Kabul. By 1835 he had extended his authority over most of Afghanistan.

His armies marched north of the Hindu Kush to subdue the Tajik, Uzbek, Turkoman, and Hazara clans. Ahmad pressed toward India, capturing Sind, Punjab, and Kashmir on the northern subcontinent. His troops destroyed the Indian cities of Lahore and Delhi. In all these conflicts, Ahmad Shah's forces killed many people and plundered the cities they captured in search of treasure.

By 1760 the weakening of the Mughal Empire allowed other powers to assert themselves on the Indian subcontinent. In northwestern India, the Sikh kingdom—made up of people who followed the Sikh religion—fought for control of Punjab. Ahmad returned again and again to the region to subdue them. His armies attacked the Sikh holy city of Amritsar, killing thousands of Sikhs and invading their places of worship.

In addition to his mastery of military tactics, Ahmad was an innovator in government. He ruled his fellow Pathans with the help of a council, whose advice he sought on important issues. Through group decision making and through fighting together to gain or hold territory, the Afghans became unified into a nation for the first time.

Unstable Monarchy

After Ahmad died in 1773, his son and declared heir, Timur Shah, succeeded him. Timur did not involve the other Pathan leaders in governing as much as his father had. As a result, many Pathan subgroups rebelled. Moreover, when Timur died in 1793 without a designated heir, all of his sons—who numbered more than 20—claimed to be his successor.

With the support of the Muhammadzai Pathan clan, Timur's fifth son, Zaman, became shah in 1793. But the difficulties over the succession and the pattern of ruling without the help of other Pathan leaders caused great instability in the royal house. Rebellions and coups occurred every few years as Timur's many sons competed for control.

In 1826 Dost Mohammad Khan, a highly placed member of the Muhammadzai Pathans, took over Kabul. In 1835 he proclaimed himself emir (ruler). Although Dost Mohammad was able to force most of Afghanistan to come under his control, two foreign powers—Russia and Great Britain—harassed the realm. The British were extending their rule over most of the Indian subcontinent. As the British advanced north and west into India, the Russians went south to spread their influence over central Asia. As a result, Afghanistan found itself caught between the colonial designs of two world powers.

First Anglo-Afghan War

Dost Mohammad allowed Russia to station a diplomat in Kabul, which was situated close to the Indian frontier. Britain felt that Russia's presence in the region threatened its holdings on the subconti-nent and demanded that Dost Mohammad remove the Russian representative from Kabul. The emir refused the demand, and in March 1838 British and Indian armies invaded Afghanistan.

This conflict, called the First Anglo-Afghan War, began a century of intermittent fighting, during which Britain and Russia attempted to conquer or weaken the small kingdoms that stood in the way of their territorial expansion. The British met with little resistance, conquering Kandahar in April 1839 and taking Ghazni in July. Kabul fell in August 1839, and the British installed Shah Shoja—one of Timur's sons—as king in place of Dost Mohammad, whom the victors took to India.

Courtesy of National Army Museum, London

In April 1842 at the end of the First Anglo-Afghan War, retreating British soldiers fought against Afghan troops to exit the Khyber Pass.

"NO YOU DON'T!"

Muhammad Akbar Khan *(above)*, **son of Dost Mohammad, led a rebellion against the pro-British Afghan ruler Shah Shoja in 1841.**

In late 1841 Muhammad Akbar Khan, the son of Dost Mohammad, led a revolt against Shah Shoja, fighting the British troops stationed in the country. The British made a costly retreat toward India, losing soldiers to Afghan fighters all along the route to the eastern city of Jalalabad. Only a few British survivors managed to leave Afghanistan in 1842. Shah Shoja was assassinated, and Dost Mohammad resumed his position as emir in 1843.

Second Anglo-Afghan War

Dost Mohammad died in 1863, and his would-be successors vied for power. One of his sons, Sher Ali Khan, attained the throne in 1868, and in 1878, after much pressure from Russia, the new king allowed a Russian diplomatic mission to be established in Kabul. This move angered the British, who demanded that a British mission—long refused by Sher Ali—should now be accepted. The demand was ignored, and in November 1878 the British-Indian army again invaded Afghanistan—a conflict known as the Second Anglo-Afghan War.

Clothed for a winter military campaign, British soldiers gather at their temporary quarters during the Second Anglo-Afghan War (1878–1879).

Sher Ali turned to Russia for help to repel the British but received no assistance. He died a few months later in Mazar-i-Sharif, and Yaqub Khan, the son and successor of Sher Ali, fled the region. In October 1879 Afghan forces retreated, and the British captured Kabul. The victors approved of placing Abdur Rahman Khan, grandson of Dost Mohammad, on the Afghan throne in 1880.

Abdur Rahman

Abdur Rahman modernized the army, suppressed crime, and reformed the nation's finances. He settled border disputes with India and Russia and curbed various local revolts by forcibly relocating more aggressive Afghan ethnic communities to other parts of the country. In 1893 Abdur Rah- man accepted a new eastern boundary that Britain's Sir Mortimer Durand had proposed. The so-called Durand Line ignored ethnic and geographic considerations and laid the foundations for later border disputes between Pakistan and Afghanistan.

The extent of Abdur Rahman's success in uniting and controlling Afghanistan was illustrated by the ease with which his son Habibollah Khan succeeded him in 1901. Habibollah carried on his father's policies, including the establishment of provincial governments, a national bureaucracy, and a permanent army.

Early Twentieth Century

Despite Afghanistan's strides toward strong nationhood, outsiders still influenced much of the nation's foreign policy at the turn of the twentieth century. In 1907, for example, Great Britain and Russia signed an agreement called the Anglo-Russian Convention. This document stated that Britain did not intend to change the political status of Afghanistan and that Russia recognized Afghanistan as outside the Russian sphere of influence. Habibollah refused to sign this treaty because he had not participated in negotiating it. Nevertheless, the Russians and the British declared the document to be in force.

During World War I (1914–1918), Habibollah cooperated with the terms of the Anglo-Russian Convention by remaining neutral in the conflict. In 1919, however, he was assassinated, and his eventual successor Amanollah Khan declared war on Great Britain in May of that year in order to break free from British intervention. The six-week war resulted in a new treaty that arranged for Britain to stop giving financial support to Afghan rulers. The document also gave Afghanistan free rein in its foreign affairs.

Amanollah introduced modernization programs and enacted a constitution in 1923. He also forcibly Westernized Afghan society and began education programs for women. In 1929 Afghans who disagreed with Amanollah's reforms attempted to overthrow him. The rebellion was put down, but Amanollah was made to give up the throne. Muhammad Nader Khan, one of the shah's former diplomatic ministers, succeeded him. Nader Shah instituted some economic reforms and united the often-warring Afghan clans. A family enemy assassinated him in 1933.

Artwork by Jim Simondet

Each king of Afghanistan had his own royal flag, which carried symbols on both the front and the back. This emblem is the front of the flag of Amanollah, who ruled from 1919 to 1929. The back of the flag bears wording in the Afghan language, which is read from right to left. For this reason, the pole on Afghan royal flags is traditionally to the right of the emblem.

Mohammad Zahir Shah

The new king, Mohammad Zahir Shah, ascended the throne in November 1933 at the age of 19. With the backing of three powerful uncles, Mohammad Zahir's transition to power went smoothly. Zahir Shah spent the first two decades of his 40-year reign under their strong influence.

Afghanistan tried to secure its independent status by joining the international League of Nations in 1934 and by establishing regional ties with the Islamic nations of Turkey and Iran (formerly Persia). Zahir Shah kept Afghanistan neutral during World War II (1939–1945) and committed himself to modernizing his country by expanding economic markets and by taking advantage of new technologies. The Helmand Valley project, for example, used the irrigation and hydroelectric potential of the Helmand River to open up new farmland in the southwest and to provide hydropower.

In 1947 Afghanistan disputed its boundary (the Durand Line) with the newly formed nation of Pakistan. Afghanistan supported Pakhtunistan—a proposed independent state for Pathans in Pakistan. If achieved, the new state would have strong ties with Pathans in Afghanistan.

In the late 1950s the government allowed the Afghan people to exercise greater political freedom. But a freer press brought out many criticisms of the government, and antigovernment political parties arose. As a result, the regime ended its relaxed policies.

Daud Khan

Within the royal family, changes also occurred. The younger generation of sons and nephews of the royal uncles—perhaps including the king—sought greater independence and a more modern outlook. When Sardar Mohammad Daud Khan, one of the king's first cousins, became prime minister in 1953, he began to modernize Afghanistan using strict measures. He

Independent Picture Service

Mohammad Zahir Shah (*pictured here in about 1960*) **was king of Afghanistan for 40 years. Deposed in 1973, the former monarch lives in exile in Italy.**

ordered women not to wear the traditional Islamic veil—a move that angered many members of the Afghan clergy—and accepted foreign loans from both the Soviet Union and the United States for improvement projects.

In addition, Daud continued to support the delicate issue of Pakhtunistan, which soured his dealings with President Ayub Khan of neighboring Pakistan. The two countries broke diplomatic relations in 1961 and closed the borders to one another's commercial traffic. This move hurt landlocked Afghanistan more than Pakistan, and the Afghan economy began to suffer seriously from the loss of trade.

Decline of Zahir Shah

In 1963 the king removed Prime Minister Daud and adopted a new constitution that established a constitutional monarchy. This change meant that the king and an

Babrak Karmal led the Parcham faction of the People's Democratic Party of Afghanistan in the 1970s and 1980s.

elected legislature would jointly rule the nation. Elections were held in September 1965 to choose members of the two-house legislature. Among the new political parties involved in the elections was the People's Democratic Party of Afghanistan (PDPA), a very liberal organization that won several parliamentary seats.

Despite the new style of government, many newspapers began to publish articles that criticized the regime's control of political affairs. Students and faculty members in Kabul demonstrated against government policies. In addition to internal difficulties, droughts threatened the country's economic stability.

Seeing these incidents as signs of an unstable government, Daud led a coup in 1973 to depose the king, who was out of the country at that time. The new leaders declared Afghanistan to be a republic (a system without a monarch), and the king remained in exile.

The 1970s

Daud introduced social and economic reforms by writing a new constitution. He eventually moved away from the socialist ideals—including government ownership of businesses and services—that his regime used to gain the support of the PDPA. He also reduced Afghanistan's financial dependence on both the Soviet Union and the United States by entering into alliances with Islamic countries. These actions and Daud's rejection of the most liberal leaders of the PDPA weakened his popular support.

The PDPA, which had strengthened its Communist ties to the Soviet Union, split into two factions. Babrak Karmal headed the Parcham faction, and Nur Mohammad Taraki led the Khalq wing of the party.

In 1977 the Parchamis and Khalqis reunited to lead an anti-Daud coup. After killing Daud, they established the Democratic Republic of Afghanistan on April 27, 1978. The new government, which supported Communist and socialist ideals, chose Taraki to fill three posts—prime minister, president of the revolutionary council, and secretary general of the PDPA. Babrak Karmal and Hafizullah Amin (a member of the Khalq faction) became deputy prime ministers.

Leaders of the new government rejected charges from other parties that the Soviet Union controlled the regime. They maintained that their policies were based on Afghan nationalism, social and economic justice, and independence in foreign affairs.

The government instituted reforms in land ownership and in women's rights. These moves threatened Afghans who valued tradition and led to violence in eastern Afghanistan in 1978.

Political rivalry reemerged between the Khalq and Parcham factions of the PDPA. Parcham members, including Karmal himself, were given diplomatic posts outside the country so that Khalqis could strengthen their control over the government without interference. In addition, the influence of deputy prime minister Hafizullah Amin grew within the administration.

Uncoordinated revolts against the increasingly Khalq-dominated government spread throughout the provinces. In February 1979 the U.S. ambassador to Afghanistan, Adolph Dubs, was killed. Thereafter, the United States severely cut back its assistance to Afghanistan, paving the way for greater Soviet influence. As revolts in rural areas continued, Amin replaced Taraki as prime minister in 1979 and sought more Soviet military aid. Amin's supporters killed Taraki, who had retained the post of president.

Soviet Takeover

Although it accepted Soviet military advice and aid, the Afghan government, in the Soviet view, was making some decisions that antagonized the Afghan people. Moreover, internal political struggles were immobilizing the administration. On December 24, 1979, Soviet troops entered Afghanistan to depose Amin. He and many of his followers died in the fighting that surrounded the presidential palace. The Soviets installed Babrak Karmal as prime minister, president of the revolutionary council, and secretary general of the PDPA.

Opposition to the Afghan socialist regime had been mounting during Amin's rule, and anti-Soviet and anti-Karmal factions spread rapidly. By the end of 1980 several groups within Afghanistan had united to resist the Soviet troops and the Soviet-supported Afghan army. Intense fighting erupted between the resistance forces—called the *mujahedeen*—and the Afghan army. The conflicts forced millions of Afghans to flee to Pakistan and Iran.

Opposition to Soviet Presence

Mujahedeen is a general name for several well-organized and often violently opposed Afghan ethnic groups. All are Muslim,

Photo by UPI/Bettmann Newsphotos

Soviet trucks traveled along a road to Kabul after Soviet troops had invaded Afghanistan in late 1979.

Members of the Afghan *mujahedeen* —resistance fighters who follow the Islamic religion—gather at one of their headquarters in Pakistan.

Photo by Bill Kish

Courtesy of A. Hollmann/UNHCR

Many Afghans fled their country during the war in the 1980s. These young refugees are being taught at a camp in eastern Iran.

Courtesy of Center for Afghanistan Studies

The mujahedeen come from many professions, although most are rural dwellers.

Supplied with U.S. weapons, rebel forces have been able to take control of mountain areas of Afghanistan during the Afghan conflict.

Courtesy of Center for Afghanistan Studies

although their approaches to Islamic ideas vary. These differences are frequently the source of interethnic conflict.

The formation of the mujahedeen may be traced to political and religious causes. The nonreligious nature of the post-Daud regimes offended many traditional Afghans. The governmental policies that were aimed at land reform and at the expansion of women's rights threatened the framework of rural life, within which most Afghans lived. The mujahedeen's opposition to the Soviet-backed government is, for the fighters, a holy war. They seek a return to age-old Islamic ideals and want to make Afghanistan an Islamic republic.

Photo © Ric Ergenbright

Dressed in traditional Islamic *chadris* (full-length coverings), women walk with their children in the capital city.

After 1980, fighting frequently occurred between the mujahedeen and Soviet-Afghan troops. The United States and China supplied sophisticated weapons to the rebels through Pakistan. By the late 1980s approximately 30,000 Soviet soldiers and about one million Afghans had died in the fighting. A further three million Afghans —or about one-fifth of the population—had moved to refugee camps in Pakistan and Iran. The leaders of the mujahedeen factions live in Peshawar, Pakistan. Some hostility exists between the leaders in exile and the Afghans who stayed in Afghanistan.

Although the Afghan regime remains in control of both Kabul and some main roads, the rest of Afghanistan is not in government hands. By the late 1980s the mujahedeen held nearly all of the mountain and border regions. Despite the advanced weaponry and training of Soviet-sponsored Afghan troops, they have been unable to control the entire country.

The Late 1980s

In 1985 Prime Minister Karmal tried to foster popular support for his regime by appointing non-Communist ethnic leaders to governmental positions. Meanwhile, the United Nations (UN) sponsored peace talks in Geneva, Switzerland, between U.S. and Soviet negotiators and between representatives of Afghanistan and Pakistan. Since the United States and the Soviet Union provided most of the weaponry used in the conflict, their participation was essential.

In May 1986, perhaps because of the poor response to Karmal's attempt to gain popular support, the Soviet Union installed Najibullah (also called Najib) as prime minister. Since the Soviet takeover, Najib had been head of KHAD, the Afghan secret police, and had won a reputation for being brutal and efficient in that post. As prime minister, Najib also made efforts to win widespread approval of the regime among the common people, but he met with little success.

The coat of arms of the Democratic Republic of Afghanistan shows an Islamic prayer niche on a green field surrounded by rays of the sun. This version of the emblem came into use in late 1987.

Artwork by Laura Westlund

According to agreements reached in April 1988, the Soviet Union withdrew some of its troops, which had been stationed in Afghanistan since 1980. In May, this convoy of Soviet tanks left Jalalabad and traveled through Kabul before going back to the Soviet Union.

UN peace efforts continued but were unsuccessful because the United States insisted that it be allowed to supply the mujahedeen with sophisticated weaponry as long as the Soviet Union sent arms to the Afghan government. In 1988 the Soviet negotiators accepted the idea that the United States could arm the Afghan rebels to the same degree and for as long as the Soviets supplied weapons to the Afghan army. Thereafter, the negotiators were able to discuss a timetable for the withdrawal of the Soviet soldiers.

Troop pullouts began in mid-1988 and will continue for nine months. No cease-fire agreement was reached, and no guarantees for the safety of departing Soviet troops were given. Indeed, the mujahedeen rejected the UN proposal, called the Geneva accord, because they were not asked to participate in the negotiations that pro-

duced it. As a result, they do not feel bound by the provisions of the accord.

Given its low level of popular support, Najibullah's regime may not last long after the Soviet withdrawal. Nevertheless, he counts about 35,000 army and secret police troops as his supporters and vows to hold on to Kabul. In addition, the various branches of the mujahedeen distrust one another almost as much as they distrust the Afghan government. This situation also diminishes the prospects for lasting peace. Without the unifying force of a foreign army on Afghan soil, the guerrilla groups may turn their aggressions on one another.

Government

In November 1987, at a gathering of Afghanistan's national assembly—called the Loya Jirgah—legislative leaders approved a new constitution. The document gave broader powers to the president. Although the new constitution made it legal for political parties other than the PDPA to exist, any additional organizations must support the goals of the PDPA.

A revolutionary council headed by the president governs the country and convenes the Loya Jirgah. The political arm of the PDPA supervises the council, but the president is usually also the head of the party, so the two groups rarely disagree.

Members of Afghanistan's supreme court, as well as lower-court judges, are appointed by the revolutionary council. Courts sometimes allow sharia, or Islamic law, to settle disputes.

Afghanistan is divided into 29 provinces, each of which has a governor who is appointed by the revolutionary council. The Afghan war, however, has weakened or eliminated most provincial authority.

In December 1987 Najibullah spoke to members of the Loya Jirgah—the Afghan legislative assembly. After approving a new constitution in November, the legislature elected Najibullah president of Afghanistan.

These Afghan children—who wear turbans and other traditional clothing—enjoy making funny faces while having their photograph taken.

3) The People

About 14.5 million people live in Afghanistan, and over three million more Afghans have moved to Pakistan and Iran since the Afghan war started in 1979. Although the nation's growth rate in 1988 was 2.4 percent, this figure is misleadingly high because the actual number of people living in the country has declined since the beginning of the Afghan conflict.

The majority of Afghans reside in rural areas in homes made of sun-dried bricks, and seasonal herders live in goatskin tents. City dwellers—who make up 15 percent of the population—often live in mud dwellings or in concrete structures. The civil war has increased the number of urban residents, who now crowd Kabul and other cities.

Ethnic Groups

Because of Afghanistan's location near international trade routes, the nation's people represent a mix of ethnic and language groups. Most Afghans belong to two main Indo-European ethnic groups—the Pathans and the Tajiks. In the north are the Uzbek and the Turkomans, who are both Turkish-speaking minorities. Small groups of Hazara—farmers of central Asian ancestry—and Nuristani, who live close to the Pakistani border, also dwell in Afghanistan.

Few of the nation's ethnic groups are contained entirely within Afghanistan, because international boundaries cut through many strong ethnic communities. In addition, old rivalries and interethnic hostilities have affected the distribution of Afghanistan's population, contributing to its lack of national identity.

Pathans make up about 40 percent of the population and are divided into many

Photo by Bill Kish

About 10 percent of Afghanistan's population are Turkomans—a group that lives in northern areas of the country.

Photo by Daniel H. Condit

This young member of the Hazara people lives near the mountains of the Hindu Kush.

Some Afghans are nomadic herders who dwell in tents and who search for seasonal grazing land for their livestock.

Photo by Bernice K. Condit

groups. The Durrani Pathans, for example, come from the Abdali clan from which the eighteenth-century leader Ahmad Shah was descended. Today subgroups of this Afghan ethnic community work in urban areas or in the countryside as farmers or herders.

Although they have established ethnic pockets throughout the nation, Pathans generally live in a broad, semicircular area in central Afghanistan. Substantial num-

bers live in Pakistan in a wide, north-south strip within 60 miles of the Afghan border.

Tajiks, Afghanistan's second largest ethnic group, make up 25 percent of the population and generally live in the northeast. Many also reside in the west near the city of Herat and in the northwest. They all speak dialects of Dari, an Indo-European language related to Farsi, which is spoken in Iran.

Veiled Hazara women wait to enter a health clinic in central Afghanistan.

Photo by Bernice K. Condit

Turkomans and Uzbek—whose territories Afghanistan and the Soviet Union share—live in the north. The Turkic language they speak is not related to the Indo-European family, and these groups represent less than 10 percent of Afghanistan's population. Most of these Turkic-speakers are farmers, although some have moved to urban centers, where they can find better schools and higher-paying jobs.

Central Afghanistan is the home of the Hazara, a Dari-speaking community of fewer than one million people. Their mountainous territory in the Hindu Kush is difficult to farm, and many Hazara have moved to Kabul, where they usually hold jobs that require little education.

A small number of Nuristani, who are mostly farmers and herders, reside in eastern Afghanistan. The Nuristani were among the first Afghans to resist the changes instituted by the Khalq regime of the late 1970s.

Mujahedeen

Although the mujahedeen (holy warriors) are not a cohesive community, they united to fight the Soviet troops that arrived in late 1979. Made up largely of seven groups —whose leaders all live in exile in Pakistan—the mujahedeen operate under an uneasy truce with one another. Traditional ethnic and language bonds distinguish the groups, each of which holds slightly different Islamic ideals.

Within Afghanistan, Ahmad Shah Massoud and his deputy Mahmud Khan are among the most respected mujahedeen leaders. Both men command guerrilla units in northeastern Afghanistan and are important members of the Jamiat-e-Islami party.

Life among the mujahedeen—who generally come from Afghanistan's farming and herding communities—is rough, with tents as shelter and with outdoor cooking sites. Their weapons are smuggled across

Since 1980, the mujahedeen have attracted a large number of followers, including some dissatisfied members of the Afghan army.

Called "the Lion of Panjsher" by his troops, Ahmad Shah Massoud has become an effective mujahedeen commander, controlling several northeastern provinces of Afghanistan.

the border from Pakistan. Guerrilla troops often walk, rather than ride, freeing their horses to carry arms and supplies. With their U.S.-supplied weapons, the mujahedeen strike at small army garrisons.

Some mujahedeen are from Afghanistan's educated minority—Massoud, for example, has a master's degree in civil engineering, and Mahmud is a former lawyer. The rebels also include farmers from rural areas and Afghan soldiers who have deserted the Afghan army. The Geneva accord of 1988 does not provide a role for the mujahedeen in future Afghan governments.

Religion

Almost all Afghans are Muslims—followers of the Islamic religion. This common feature, however, does not mean that they all belong to the same religious division of Islam or that they share identical beliefs.

Islam began in Saudi Arabia in the seventh century A.D., when the prophet Muhammad began to preach a faith based on submission to one god—Allah. All Muslims were considered equal in their allegiance to Allah. Armies of Muslim warriors spread the religion, bringing it to Afghanistan in about 700.

Soon after Muhammad's death in 632, the faith split into factions. The main subgroups called themselves Sunnis (those who follow the traditional Islamic practices of the Sunna, or example of Muhammad) and Shiites, who accept the guidelines of Ali, Muhammad's son-in-law. Shiites regard Ali as the prophet's true successor, and they support only those religious leaders who are descendants of Muhammad's family. Sunnis, on the other hand, elect their Islamic leaders. Within Afghanistan, most Muslims belong to the Sunni sect, although the Hazara are Shiites.

No matter what the sect, Islam requires that its believers fulfill certain obligations. Among these duties are daily prayer, fasting during the holy month of Ramadan, and making donations to the poor. In addition, male Muslims must try to visit the holy city of Mecca in Saudi Arabia at least once in their lifetime.

Islam has played a vital role in the Afghan conflict. The mujahedeen, who are committed to Islamic ideals, are trying to establish Afghanistan as an Islamic republic. If a new government emerges after the withdrawal of Soviet forces, Islamic leaders could become important in maintaining national unity.

Language and Literature

Dari (also called Afghan Farsi) and Pashto —both members of the Indo-European family of languages—are the two official languages of Afghanistan. Dari is the most common tongue, although the government

Among the Islamic religion's most important figures is Ali—the son-in-law of Muhammad, who founded the faith in the seventh century. This mosque in Mazar-i-Sharif contains a tomb commemorating Ali and thus has become an important place of religious pilgrimage.

A sign in the Dari language, which is the most common tongue in Afghanistan, describes jobs that a local mechanic can do.

has given preference to Pashto in an effort to increase its usage. Both languages use the same alphabet and are read from right to left. People in the north close to the Soviet border speak Uzbek and other Turkic dialects that belong to the Ural-Altaic language family.

Spoken poetry is Afghanistan's most important literary form. Many of the cultures that flourished in Afghanistan encouraged the writing and memorizing of verse, and modern Afghans can recite works by poets of bygone eras. The poems often express themes of unattainable love, or they glorify the warrior spirit.

Most modern Afghan authors—who produce works in Dari, Pashto, and Turkic—

write poetry rather than novels or other Western-style prose. Until his entry into politics, however, Nur Mohammad Taraki had a growing reputation as a Dari novelist. With a small literate population, Afghanistan has used its educated minority to administer the government as well as to enrich its literary life. As a result, many of the nation's major poets have served as ambassadors, diplomats, or cabinet ministers.

Education

Following the 1979 revolution, the Afghan government—supported financially by the Soviet Union—began to expand education.

Courtesy of Center for Afghanistan Studies

Carrying his books and a small blackboard, a young Afghan makes his way to school. Because of the Afghan conflict, many parts of the country lack teachers, school materials, and educational facilities. As a result, the number of school-aged Afghans who attend classes has dropped.

A mother in a war-torn section of Afghanistan cradles her starving child. War and drought—both causes of a decrease in the food supply—have made malnutrition more common among young children.

Laws were enacted that required all children between the ages of 7 and 10 to attend school. In the mid-1980s, however, few teachers and elementary schools existed in the country, and secondary schools operated only in Kabul and in provincial capitals. More than 90 percent of the population over the age of 25 have had no formal schooling. Only 33 percent of Afghan males and 6 percent of females can read or write.

Where schools and teachers do exist, however, instructors use the local language, and textbooks are written in Dari, Pashto, Uzbek, and other dialects. Because of the government's close relationship with the Soviet Union, Afghan students have been sent—some say they have been forced to go—to the Soviet Union to receive more educational training.

Technical, art, business, and medical schools exist for higher education, and Kabul University, founded in 1932, offers courses in medicine, science, agriculture, engineering, law, political science, and economics. The University of Nangarhar in Jalalabad was founded in 1962, and a vocational school opened in Kabul in 1968.

Health

Two main factors—the Afghan war and drought—have affected health statistics in Afghanistan in recent years. In addition,

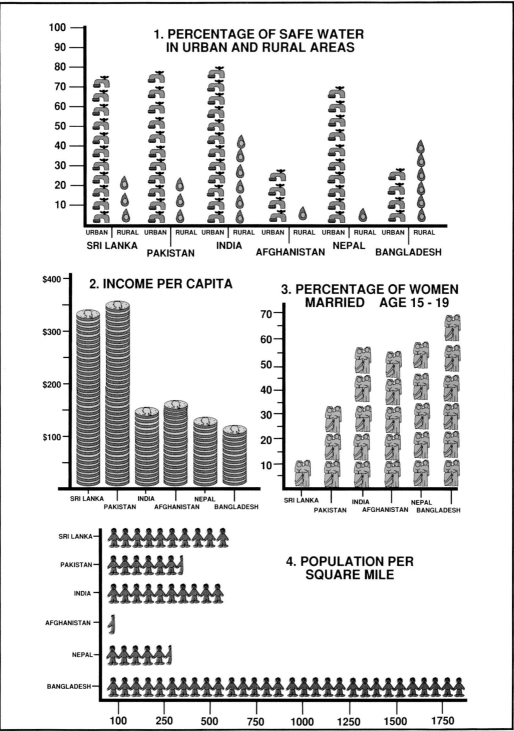

1. PERCENTAGE OF SAFE WATER IN URBAN AND RURAL AREAS

URBAN | RURAL — SRI LANKA
URBAN | RURAL — PAKISTAN
URBAN | RURAL — INDIA
URBAN | RURAL — AFGHANISTAN
URBAN | RURAL — NEPAL
URBAN | RURAL — BANGLADESH

2. INCOME PER CAPITA

SRI LANKA
PAKISTAN
INDIA
AFGHANISTAN
NEPAL
BANGLADESH

3. PERCENTAGE OF WOMEN MARRIED   AGE 15 - 19

SRI LANKA
PAKISTAN
INDIA
AFGHANISTAN
NEPAL
BANGLADESH

4. POPULATION PER SQUARE MILE

SRI LANKA
PAKISTAN
INDIA
AFGHANISTAN
NEPAL
BANGLADESH

100 250 500 750 1000 1250 1500 1750

Artwork by Mindy A. Rabin

Depicted in this chart are factors relating to the standard of living in six countries in southern Asia. Information taken from "1987 World Population Data Sheet," "The World's Women: A Profile," and "Children of the World" compiled by the Population Reference Bureau, Washington, D.C.

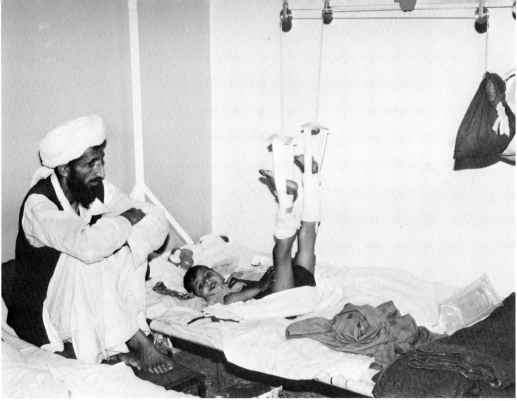

In a refugee hospital in Pakistan, Afghans recover from wounds inflicted by gunfire and bombs.

treatable diseases, such as malaria, measles, and tuberculosis, continue to afflict the population. As a result, among Asian countries Afghanistan has the highest death rate (24 people in every 1,000), the highest infant death statistic under the age of one (183 per 1,000), and the lowest life expectancy (39 years).

The government has tried to increase the number of clinics and health professionals, but new facilities and personnel tend to cluster in Kabul and other cities. In addition, wounded mujahedeen and their families cannot seek national health care, because they are rebels. Most of the wounded travel to rebel bases in Pakistan for treatment. Children have become casualties of the war, and wounds from mines and bombs have left many youngsters crippled and maimed.

Drought, which has affected Afghanistan several times in the last two decades, continues to deplete food sources. The war, which disrupts the agricultural economy, further decreases the food supply and makes malnutrition a major cause of disease and death.

Food and Clothing

When food is plentiful, pilau—rice mixed with meat and vegetables—is served throughout Afghanistan. Saffron, a spice sometimes added during cooking, turns the rice a bright yellow. Pilau is such a common dish that the word has come to mean food in general. *Bolani,* resembling spicy vegetable pies, and *korma,* a vegetable side dish, are other favorites.

Afghan bread, called *nan,* is usually made of whole wheat flour, although other grains—barley, corn, or millet—are also used. Cooks bake some breads in ovens built into the ground and form other loaves into flat rounds that are fried on griddles. Desserts in Afghanistan are sweet and rich, and fresh fruit is also popular. *Jelabi* (deep-fried pieces of wheat bread coated with syrup) and gur (molasses lumps) sometimes complete a meal.

49

Photo by Daniel H. Condit

A streetside vendor offers freshly baked *nan*—Afghan bread—for sale in Kabul.

Both black and green teas accompany meals and are often spiced with cardamom. Some Afghans soak a lump of sugar in tea before eating the sweet for refreshment, or they may drink the tea through a sugar cube.

Afghan men and women generally wear loose-fitting clothing—including cotton shirts and baggy trousers. Women also dress in long skirts made of brightly dyed cloth. Heavy coats become a necessity when the weather turns cold in November.

Men often wear turbans—long pieces of cloth wrapped around the head—or turbanlike caps. The turbans may be tied in distinctive ways to indicate ethnic affiliation. For women, the traditional head covering is a shawl, which they can pull across their faces to hide themselves from strangers. In keeping with Islamic ideals of modesty, some Afghan women wear the *chadri* —a long, hooded robe that reveals only the wearer's eyes.

The Arts and Recreation

Traditional music and folk dances play a major role in Afghanistan's cultural life. In

Photo by Bill Kish

Wearing turbans, these Afghan men enjoy a meal of salad and kebabs—skewered chunks of meat and vegetables grilled over an open fire.

In Afghanistan, the word pilau has come to mean food in general, although traditional pilaus are a mixture of rice, herbs, and vegetables.

a population that generally cannot read or write, these musical and visual forms preserve historical and ethnic ties. The *attan* is a Pathan war dance that reenacts the lifestyle of Pathan fighters. Performers form a large circle, quickening their movements as the tempo of the music increases.

Ballads, dances, and stories are performed to the accompaniment of tradi-tional Afghan instruments, including the *dhol* (a drum), the tamboura (a stringed gourd), and the surnay (a wind instrument). Craftspeople, particularly in rural areas, produce rugs, leather goods, and gold and silver jewelry using age-old techniques.

Recreation in Afghanistan ranges from picnicking to spirited games of *buzkashi*,

Dancers perform the *attan*—a Pathan dance—before the beginning of a game of buzkashi.

in which dozens of horsemen try to pick up the headless carcass of a calf and carry it to a goal. Buzkashi is most often played in northern Afghanistan and affords participants an opportunity to display high-quality horsemanship. Wrestling is also a popular sport, and game rules allow players to grab opponents' arms and clothing but never their legs. At the end of a match, wrestlers may be wearing little more than shreds of fabric.

Western-style sports—including soccer, field hockey, and golf—were introduced in the mid-twentieth century. But the Olympic sports in which Afghans have excelled —wrestling and weight-lifting—remain related to traditional competitions that Afghans pursue.

Using brightly colored wool, Afghan craftspeople knot rugs by hand according to beautiful geometric designs.

Courtesy of Center for Afghanistan Studies

Independent Picture Service

Buzkashi—a rugged sport played mostly in northern Afghanistan—attracts skilled riders. Each player vies to hold on to the carcass of a headless calf while racing at full speed toward a goal.

Accompanied by a young Afghan, a pair of oxen pull a device that threshes a field of hay.

4) The Economy

Afghanistan is one of the world's least economically developed nations, and since 1979 the Afghan war has slowed the limited progress that was occurring. The conflict has also caused two distinct economies to evolve. Each mirrors the particular area of control dominated by the warring groups.

One sector focuses on Kabul and other urban areas, which have the advantages of established industries and sources of electrical power. The other economy—beyond the authority of the Afghan government—lies in the countryside, where small-scale farming supports most families.

As a result of this economic split, urban Afghanistan has become extremely dependent on the Soviet Union for food and other goods. Rural Afghans, on the other hand, have received help through Pakistan from Western nations but will face hard times if the fighting continues.

Agriculture

Despite some industrial development, Afghanistan remains primarily a rural society in which farming and livestock raising are the main livelihoods. Only 12 percent of the land is suitable for crops, and only about 2 percent is regularly cultivated.

53

Farmers use the remaining arable acreages as pastureland.

Because of the nation's largely mountainous and dry terrain, most crops are grown in the fertile plains and valleys near sources of water or with the help of irrigation. In recent decades, the government has launched agricultural projects in the southwest that use the waters of the Helmand River for irrigation. The projects have transformed some desert areas into productive farmland.

The Afghan war has seriously eroded the nation's agricultural sector. Fighting has caused farm laborers to flee to the cities or to leave Afghanistan, and bombings have destroyed crops and irrigation systems. Nevertheless, there are widely differing views on Afghanistan's present agricultural situation.

The Afghan government maintains that, in general, crop volumes have risen substantially since the mid-1970s and that acreages have expanded. Other analysts—mostly in Pakistan and the United States—disagree with these positive views. They say that large amounts of imported food and high prices for locally grown food are evidence of agricultural failures. These observers estimate that wheat production has decreased by 80 percent, that corn crops have dropped 77 percent, and that volumes of other cereals have declined by 74 percent. Hardest hit, experts believe, is the cotton crop, which they estimate has dropped by 88 percent.

Wheat has traditionally been Afghanistan's main crop and most important food. The government estimated that Afghan farms produced about three million tons

Farmers in this village of northern Afghanistan employ terracing and irrigation to get the most agricultural use from their land.

Afghanistan's cotton crop has declined in recent years. Here, a cotton fluffer plumps the fibers that will stuff a mattress.

A group of Hazara farmers winnows grain by throwing the stalks in the air and allowing the wind to carry away the light husks. The kernels, which will be ground into flour, fall to the ground.

Grapes grow well in Afghanistan's hot summer weather and are used to produce wine for export.

Independent Picture Service

Supplied with the skins of locally raised animals, this tanner scrapes a hide — an early step in the process of making leather.

Independent Picture Service

Thirsty Karakul sheep *(above)* arrive at a stream in northern Afghanistan. Once these animals are fully mature, their skins become a valuable source of income. A Karakul herd *(right)* awaits inspection for quality at a government installation.

of wheat annually in the mid-1980s. Other important crops are cotton, barley, maize (corn), and rice. Fruit and nuts—both fresh and preserved—remain important export crops. Farmers plant wheat and corn throughout Afghanistan, and they cultivate barley in the highlands. Rice is planted in the west and in the provinces of Kunduz and Baghlan, and cotton fields thrive near Mazar-i-Sharif.

Livestock hold an important place in rural communities. Farmers raise animals for their meat, milk, and wool. In addition, cattle, goats, and donkeys perform vital functions as draft (load-pulling) animals on the farms. In northern Afghanistan, the Karakul sheep is the most valuable breed, and the skins of these animals are highly prized. The Karakul pelt industry is one of the few in Afghanistan to earn substantial foreign income.

OPIUM POPPIES

Although they are illegal to grow, opium poppies—from which the addictive drugs heroin and opium are made—thrive in eastern Afghanistan. The poppies are the nation's biggest money earner, and, except during the drought in 1984, harvests have increased in recent years. Most cultivation occurs in the provinces of Nangarhar, Badakhshan, and Paktia.

In 1986 Afghan farmers produced 800 tons of raw opium, which were refined in laboratories in Nangarhar province. This region is next to Pakistan's North-West Frontier Province, where dozens of laboratories also process Afghan poppies into heroin. Afghanistan's heroin is exported to India, to Iran, and to markets in the United States and Europe. The nation's drug traffic is believed to bring in as much as $100 million annually.

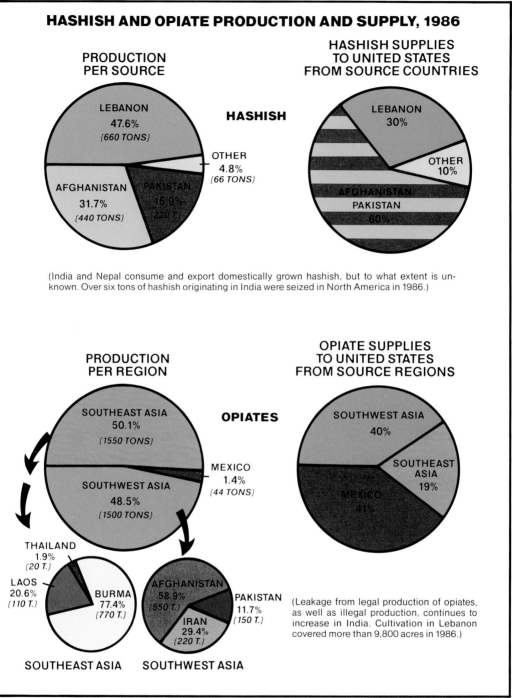

HASHISH AND OPIATE PRODUCTION AND SUPPLY, 1986

PRODUCTION PER SOURCE

HASHISH

HASHISH SUPPLIES TO UNITED STATES FROM SOURCE COUNTRIES

LEBANON
47.6%
(660 TONS)

OTHER
4.8%
(66 TONS)

AFGHANISTAN
31.7%
(440 TONS)

PAKISTAN
15.9%
(220 T.)

LEBANON
30%

OTHER
10%

AFGHANISTAN/
PAKISTAN
60%

(India and Nepal consume and export domestically grown hashish, but to what extent is unknown. Over six tons of hashish originating in India were seized in North America in 1986.)

PRODUCTION PER REGION

OPIATES

OPIATE SUPPLIES TO UNITED STATES FROM SOURCE REGIONS

SOUTHEAST ASIA
50.1%
(1550 TONS)

MEXICO
1.4%
(44 TONS)

SOUTHWEST ASIA
48.5%
(1500 TONS)

SOUTHWEST ASIA
40%

SOUTHEAST
ASIA
19%

MEXICO
41%

THAILAND
1.9%
(20 T.)

LAOS
20.6%
(110 T.)

BURMA
77.4%
(770 T.)

AFGHANISTAN
58.9%
(550 T.)

PAKISTAN
11.7%
(150 T.)

IRAN
29.4%
(220 T.)

SOUTHEAST ASIA

SOUTHWEST ASIA

(Leakage from legal production of opiates, as well as illegal production, continues to increase in India. Cultivation in Lebanon covered more than 9,800 acres in 1986.)

Artwork by Elizabeth Pilon

These pie charts depict data about both the production and U.S. supplies of two kinds of drugs. Hashish is a substance taken from the *Cannabis sativa* plant, which also is a source of marijuana. Opiates are drugs that come from opium poppies *(Papaver somniferum)*, mostly in the refined forms of opium and heroin. The production pies *(left)* cover the percentages estimated to be manufactured by each country or region. The pies depicting U.S. supplies *(right)* illustrate only percentages that arrive in the United States. They do not include amounts used within source countries or regions, nor do they illustrate percentages that go to other parts of the world. Data taken from the *NNICC Report, 1985–1986* compiled by the U.S. Drug Enforcement Administration, Washington, D.C.

Mining and Forestry

Mining experts have discovered large underground deposits of natural gas near Shibarghan, which lies about 75 miles west of Mazar-i-Sharif. With Soviet assistance, Afghan governments have been developing drilling facilities in the region since 1967. Two fields in Jowzjan province are now major producers of natural gas, and their plants are capable of both storage and refining. Pipelines deliver nearly all of the gas to the Soviet Union.

Afghanistan also has proven oil reserves of roughly 100 million barrels in the provinces of Faryab and Jowzjan. With Soviet aid, oil fields and refineries will soon produce substantial amounts of fuel.

Coal deposits are located on the northern slopes of the Hindu Kush, and miners extract the mineral from fields in the provinces of Baghlan and Balkh. Afghanistan also has deposits of other minerals, including chromite (from which chrome is made), iron ore, copper, silver, and rock salt. The country's underdeveloped road network and difficult terrain hamper mining of these reserves.

Afghanistan is the world's leading supplier of lapis lazuli, a blue, semiprecious stone. The center of lapis mining is in the province of Badakhshan, especially within its remote sections in the Hindu Kush.

Forests cover about 7,300 square miles of Afghanistan, mostly in the eastern part of the country and on the south-facing slopes of the Hindu Kush. The eastern stands are primarily evergreens, which provide wood for the construction industry. Other trees, especially oaks, are burned as fuel. Pistachio trees, whose nuts are a major export item, grow on the northern slopes of the Hindu Kush. Gum

Photo by Bernice K. Condit

Using a cart called a *karachi,* workers haul a supply of wooden poles to a building site in Charikar, eastern Afghanistan.

Courtesy of Jack A. Hill

Three generations of Afghan craftspeople weave the design of an Afghan rug by hand.

resin is harvested from trees and is exported to India. Virtually no national reforestation projects exist, and the limited amount of forested land is shrinking.

Industry

Afghanistan's industrial sector is still in an early stage of development. Most of the nation's factories are in Kabul, and production is based on agricultural raw materials —which have been increasingly hard to get since the Afghan conflict began in 1979. Cotton and woolen textiles, leather goods, furniture, glass, bicycles, prefabricated houses, and plastics continue to be the country's most important manufactured products.

The Soviet Union has constructed and equipped machine shops capable of manufacturing motor parts. Textile mills operate at Pul-i-Khumri and Balkh, and a factory that extracts oil from seeds has

been established at Gulbahar. The Soviets have outfitted a sugar beet plant at Baghlan, and other manufacturing firms produce leather and machine-made carpets.

Traditional handwoven items continue to contribute to the total manufacturing output. About 10 percent of Afghanistan's foreign income is earned from the sale of pure wool carpets. Weaving is generally a home-based industry centered in the northern and northwestern provinces. Most of the hand-knotted carpets go to Europe and Iran.

Transportation and Energy

With few navigable rivers and no railroads, Afghanistan must rely primarily on highway transport. In the 1960s the Soviet Union and the United States each funded the construction of separate highway networks between cities along Afghanistan's northern and eastern borders.

Over 11,000 miles of roads crisscross the country, but only about 2,000 miles of them are paved. Most roads are in poor repair, and bridges are often washed out by overflowing rivers. Although thousands of commercial vehicles operate in Afghanistan, camels and donkeys are commonly used as draft animals. Rural Afghans still cherish horses as symbols of status and as forms of transport.

Afghanistan is one of the few nations in the world that has no national railway. In 1982, however, the Amu Darya Bridge in northern Afghanistan opened. It eventually will bring Soviet track into the country. A 120-mile line is planned between Termez in the Soviet Union and Pul-i-Khumri.

Built with U.S. help, Kabul Airport has been expanded with Soviet aid. Provincial all-weather airports exist at Herat, Kunduz, Jalalabad, and Mazar-i-Sharif. Ariana

Courtesy of W. Campbell-Notar

Along the Khyber Pass, which connects Afghanistan to Pakistan, a sign designates the roads for motorized *(right)* and nonmotorized forms of transportation.

Courtesy of W. Campbell-Notar

As it twists through the mountains, this paved, two-lane road provides the main overland link between the cities of Kabul and Jalalabad.

Afghan Airlines operates regular services to Moscow and Tashkent in the Soviet Union, to Prague in Czechoslovakia, and to New Delhi in India. The domestic national airline, Bakhtar Afghan Airlines, serves major airfields within Afghanistan.

Hydroelectric plants generate about 75 percent of Afghanistan's electricity. The government has constructed several dams on the Helmand and Kabul rivers, but seasonal fluctuations in water flow hamper full use of their energy potential. Hydropower stations also lie in the region between Kabul and Jalalabad, with further installations at Naghlu, Mahipar, Pul-i-Khumri, and Kandahar. The rest of Afghanistan's electricity comes from thermal power— heat-generating plants that are fueled by coal or petroleum products.

The Afghan war has limited the supply of electricity, which only about 10 percent of the population receive under normal peacetime circumstances. Electric power and transmission lines are popular rebel targets, and the residents of Kabul experience frequent blackouts. Other cities, such as Kandahar and Herat, often have electrical shortages, and sometimes no power is available at all.

Afghanistan's rugged terrain isolates the country and hampers its economic development.

The Future

Afghanistan's physical isolation—imposed by mountains, deserts, and its landlocked location—has contributed to the nation's position as one of Asia's least industrialized countries. Afghan governments of the 1960s and 1970s tried to attract foreign investments to upgrade the nation's roads, industries, and economy.

Both the United States and the Soviet Union helped in a variety of ways—by expanding the transportation network, by

A member of the mujahedeen carries some of the sophisticated weaponry supplied by the United States and China.

This young Afghan refugee and her family live in Pakistan, where millions of Afghan citizens fled after war broke out in 1979.

At a rally in support of the mujahedeen, a crowd of turbaned Afghans confronts the problems of their war-torn country.

introducing new agricultural technology, and by granting loans to finance additional improvements. Until its present political problems are solved, however, Afghanistan will be unable to revive even the slow economic progress that it had achieved before the civil war began.

Much of Afghanistan's future depends on how the Afghan government functions without the backing of the Soviet army. Estimates suggest that only 5 percent of the population actively support the government, and the mujahedeen have vowed to continue to fight for an Islamic republic. Meanwhile, millions of Afghan refugees in Pakistan and Iran await a peaceful solution to the conflict in their homeland.

Index